To my wife, Jacqueline Rose, for walking beside me on our journey into grace. When I drift back to performance, she softly whispers in my ear, "But what if ... grace?"

HOW GRACE *Sets Us Free*
FROM THE PERFORMANCE MINDSET

LIVING
UNDER
the
INFLUENCE

TODD W. SCHULTZ

LUCIDBOOKS

ISBN: 978-1-63296-828-9
eISBN: 978-1-63296-829-6

SPECIAL THANKS

Thank you to my pastor, Justin Grunewald, for his influence on my grace story. God challenged my performance mindset years before I met Justin, but it was under his leadership that God helped me comprehend that my freedom could come by grace. The transparent manner that Justin shares his story inspired me to write mine with the same degree of transparency and honesty. Many of the lessons I have communicated in this book have been influenced by what Justin learned about grace through the unfolding of his own journey. Thank you, Justin, for being used by God to continue my reconsideration of grace.

TABLE OF CONTENTS

INTRODUCTION

My wife Jackie loves going to the movies. In fact, I call her a movie connoisseur. When we married, she hooked me into going to the movies too. I enjoy watching a good movie, but she loves everything about the experience. I now appreciate the experience almost as much as she does. Early on in our marriage, I learned that there is a perfect spot to watch a movie in the theater. I did not know that. And there are rules to follow. Each person can eat their popcorn before the movie, but there is no eating during the movie. I must admit that she has changed somewhat on that rule, and I still believe eating popcorn during the movie makes it better. Oh, and once the movie starts, it is a mortal sin to talk. It took a little time to learn all the rules, but today I can say we love sharing this experience together.

The only thing that rivals going to the movies is the current trend called binge-watching. Jackie loves to binge-watch a television series. Me? Not so much. She will stay up into the wee hours of the morning to follow the suspense and drama of a spellbinding plot while I doze off happily in my recliner much earlier in the evening.

Like movie-going grew on me, so has binge-watching. I don't have the attention span to watch a whole series in one night, but I have come to love the anticipation of what happens next in a twist-and-turn plot. I realized recently that binge-watching is actually not something new to me. I think I have been a television binge-watcher for most of my life. My normal pattern is to flick on the television when I walk into a room whether I intend to watch it or not. I also go to sleep more easily when I'm watching television.

I attribute my television binge-watching behavior to the start of my grace story. I grew up in a church that equated personal holiness with a person's outward appearance and entertainment choices. The people in that church had a deep desire to please God and experience his presence, but their desire led them to interpret Scripture in a way that reflected a performance mindset. Men and women were taught to wear certain types of clothes to maintain modesty and holiness. The television was the devil's box, and sports were forbidden. These standards were reinforced on a regular basis, so personal effort and constant evaluations of behavior became the norm for me.

When I was growing up in this church, I felt a deep desire at a very young age to follow God. Even before I became a Christian, my personality was bent toward living a life that pleased God. I attribute my desire for God to his grace and not my ambitions. If left to myself, my tendency has always leaned toward self-effort. The constant reinforcement of living with the "right" behaviors and my desire to please God left me destined to struggle with a performance mindset.

As I grew into my young adult years, I became more aware of my walk with God. I continued to assess how I was living on a regular basis. I periodically made the necessary changes that I thought would please God. Church was part of my regular routine, just as I was taught as a child. I prayed and read the

Scriptures. In my early 20s, I began to serve in ministry as a teacher and preacher. I enjoyed success early in ministry. For all practical purposes, it looked like everything was going well.

But there was something deeper going on in my heart. Ministry became a major part of my identity, probably to a fault. The more success I experienced in ministry, the more I believed I was pleasing God. However, when I struggled in ministry, I felt like a failure not only in the church but also in God's eyes. That pattern of life became part of who I was as a believer and minister in the church. Privately, I worked for a certain type of life that I believed honored God. It was a cyclical pattern with feelings of success and failure, all connected to how I was doing in ministry. When the ministry was thriving, I found it easier to order my life in a godly way. But when I was struggling in the church, I questioned God's love for me and whether I could be successful enough to please him. Shame from failing to live a life pleasing to God and the guilt of never knowing if my life was ever good enough fueled this vicious cycle of performance.

Very few people knew of my internal struggle associated with the performance mindset. The more changes I made to my outward life, the more I struggled to hit the mark of personal holiness. The more I read Scripture and prayed to distract myself from behaviors I wanted to avoid, the worse the guilt and shame seemed to grow over the years. This pattern vacillated between behaviors I relentlessly tried to suppress and others like prayer that I was striving to improve.

This performance mentality followed me into the darkest days of my life when I endured the death of my marriage through an unexpected divorce for which I was completely unprepared.

The divorce ended my involvement in ministry, at least the way I had known it in my 20s and 30s. I saw myself as a failed preacher, husband, and father. For 10 long years after the divorce, I was a very angry, bitter man. I made life for my family very difficult. I had lost who I was due to the loss of my ministry, and everyone around me suffered for it.

My performance mindset reflected how I viewed God and myself. The effects of divorce convinced me that it was God's judgment because of my personal failure in ministry and in my family. I could see no hope in the years following the divorce because I did not view God through a lens of grace, and I didn't believe that he saw me through a lens of grace. My belief about God was influenced by the legalism of my church background and my intense desire to demonstrate my love for him by how I lived my life. While I now know that this desire was a bit misguided, striving to please God reinforced my sense of failure evidenced by the end of my marriage.

But God was patient with me. Through ten years marked by selfishness and anger, he gently led me. He used my new role as a special educator to begin healing the wounds in my heart. Little by little, he revealed how his grace had been at work all along, reshaping my view of him—not as a harsh judge, but as a loving Father—and transforming how I saw myself: not as a failure, but as someone being restored. There were a few times during those 10 years when I sensed the closeness of God. The turning point toward grace came when God pointed out who I was becoming—an angry and wounded man. I began to recognize the useless nature of trying to perform for God while never feeling as if I could do anything good enough to please him.

That personal epiphany led me to a two-year journey where I asked for forgiveness from every person I had hurt along the way. That period became more significant than just healing those relationships. God used many of those conversations to soften my heart to receive his grace. As I began to grasp the influence of grace, I read everything I could find about grace as I learned the implications of God's love for me despite the depths of my own brokenness. This book represents what God has taught me thus far about what it means to live under the influence of grace.

Grace and the Performance Mindset

What do I mean by grace and the performance mindset? Grace acts as the influence on our Christian lives that has everything to do with God's choice to relate to us from a heart of favor and love. His grace (Greek: *charis*) represented the first decision he ever made for us to live under his influence. Paul wrote that "grace was given us in Christ Jesus *before* the beginning of time" (emphasis added) (2 Tim. 1:9). Before the recorded beginning in Genesis, God chose to relate to us differently than anything else he created. It is under the influence of his grace that he considers us his people, the chosen ones, his special possession (1 Pet. 2:9–10).

His decision to relate to us by grace was not one he had to force. His decision to relate to us with faithfulness and steadfast love came from the nature of who he is as God. The Bible describes him as "the God of all grace" (1 Pet. 5:10), which means he chose us before time was first recorded to relate to us with perfect favor and eternal love because that is who he has always been.

It is his nature to choose for our good much like parents care for their own misguided and imperfect children. We enjoy our children, especially when they are young and see us as heroes. We love them unconditionally even when they transform into teenagers with attitude and angst. We protect our little ones even as they rebel. We hold them when they hurt. We nurture them to help them grow. We provide for them even when they are selfish, not because they deserve it but because of who they are as our children and who we are as their parents. God already made the decision to lean into us in much the same way with eyes of love, words and deeds of kindness, and the protection and provision of a parent untainted by the effects of their own imperfections. That is favor, and that is how God regards us.

While grace influences how God chooses to relate to us, many of us unfortunately listen to a different influencer called the performance mindset. It represents our efforts to define God or ourselves apart from his love for us and out of a sense of obligation to him. This book is written for all who want to know God, but whose efforts to know him became lost in their misunderstanding of who he is as the God of all grace.

While the performance mindset looks different for each person, depending on the nature of the journey, there are some common characteristics that we share. Performance-minded people place a high value on personal effort. Self-effort becomes our mechanism to please God. The decisions we make for God may differ, but the source of that effort usually comes from a deep love for God.

The performance-minded person often equates personal circumstances, whether good or bad, with how God must feel about them. If things are going well in life, we think God is pleased with us. If we have struggles, we conclude we're not doing enough or doing something wrong. We remember our past mistakes as an indictment that speaks louder than our desire to show God how much we love him. Therefore, we make changes to our personal life to find approval from God and sometimes, depending on our brand of performance, approval from others.

The performance mentality has a lot to do with outward behavior. Most of us who are caught in this trap believe there are certain behaviors we need to continue—prayer, reading the Bible, church attendance—or ones we need to stop such as drinking, cursing, watching pornography, or binging on food. We place a lot of importance on physical ways to measure how well we love God or how much we think God loves us. The makeup of each list depends on the value we place on certain behaviors. But make no mistake. The behaviors we choose are influenced by our past experiences and reflective of our idea of what it means to be a Christian. The focus of life becomes what we should or should not do. We believe that living better will qualify us to be loved more by God.

Finally, performance-minded people usually live with doubts and questions about our own faith in God. We question how God may feel about us related to what we have done or not done. Our past failures encourage many of our questions. Trauma may influence our mistrust of God as a perfect Father, or the mistakes we make today can deepen our doubts about tomorrow. Those emotions cause us to cycle back and forth between our efforts to do more things for God or totally abandon the idea of pursuing him all together. In either case, an introduction to grace can open the door to a whole new life with God.

The Purpose of This Book

This book represents my journey to grace. I became a Christian when I was a teenager, but it was not until after seminary training and preaching many years that I began to understand what I had been missing by underestimating the influence of grace. I found that my preoccupation with what I did for God always left me questioning if I had done enough. Even though I privately struggled with those doubts for years, I held on to the belief that God was continuing his work in me that started the day I came to Christ. However, those doubts along the way clouded the significance of the moment I put my faith in Jesus.

The beliefs I have held about God over the years have deep roots in my heart. My performance mentality reinforced certain myths that influenced what I believed and how I lived. I have met countless people over the years who believed the same things I did about God and themselves, keeping them bound in the same endless circle of striving to please him. Certain myths that fuel these inaccurate beliefs play out in an if-then thought pattern as we clamor for the imaginary key to be found acceptable to God. In each chapter of this book, I propose how grace offers an alternative way of thinking to some of the following myths that tend to shape our perspective of God:

- If I pray and read the Bible more, then God will change how I feel about myself.
- If I live a holy life and make good choices, then God will be pleased with me.
- If I have a messy life, then God will not choose or accept me.
- If I clean up my act first, then God can use me in his kingdom.
- If I become a better person, then God will bless me with a better life.

My aim is not to convince you that grace is the better way to think than what these myths suggest. I simply want to introduce grace as the influence that God has always intended for our Christian lives. I am still learning how grace can set us free from the performance mindset. Even though I am very mindful that I am still a work in progress, I am done trying to prove how much I love God by what I do. I simply want to live loved by God and as a result to love others well from the overflow of his love for me.

If you are tired of constantly trying to please God or just willing to take another look at grace, then I invite you to join me on my journey for a short time. I invite you to consider an alternative way to think about God and yourself as one of his followers. That alternative way of thinking is grace.

CHAPTER 1

Myth: If I pray and read the Bible more, then God will change how I feel about myself.

What if grace means ...

Your worth comes not from doing but from being favored.

There are pivotal influences that shape our spiritual outlook, and those influences impact how we think about God. For instance, our relationship with our parents can influence our ability or inability to see God as a loving Father. Our church experiences may impact decisions about whether we decide to go to church or not. Trauma can raise questions about whether God is truly the loving God he claims to be. Or, in my case, church teaching and the trauma of divorce can reinforce a misunderstanding of how God relates to us. Living under the influence of grace doesn't erase any of these experiences, but it does impact whether we break free from their hold on our lives or not. By grace, those experiences can form the story of our lives without defining our life in Christ—they can make up our grace stories.

How we live and the decisions we make depend in large part on the things that influence us. Our experiences may be different, but anytime we respond to or define God or ourselves apart from the story he is forming in us, we fall into the performance mindset trap. If we seek to please God by how we live, we get trapped in thought patterns that focus our attention on things we do for God. We characterize the quality of our spiritual lives by how well we are performing certain holy tasks. For example, we pray or read the Bible because that is how we grow closer to God. Or we attend a small group and go to church because we have been taught to not give up "meeting together, as some are in the habit of doing" (Heb. 10:25). While nothing about this is inherently wrong, practices like these can become the end rather than the means to the end for people with a performance mindset.

This was the case for me. Since I believed that holiness reflected how well I was living, I regularly scrutinized my behaviors and memorialized those patterns that had changed and those that had not. Early in my Christian life, I read my Bible regularly and used prayer lists to keep track of prayer requests. Even later, during those 10 years of wandering after the divorce when I refused to go to church, I ended up again finding my spot in the church pew. On the surface, I was still doing everything the way I was taught, but I was as far from God as a person could be. Why was that?

I eventually discovered the problem with my discipline-based approach to the Christian life. It was based on the assumption that I had what it takes to live a well-lived life. Consequently, I always found myself scrutinizing how I was living and keeping track of whether prayers were being answered or not. What I did and how well I prayed became the focus of my activities. Reading the Bible and attending church were physical benchmarks to measure my faithfulness to God. However, praying and reading my Bible more and doing things like watching TV less never seemed to make me feel closer to God. That's because the list became my focus, and less television time became my goal. The performance mindset kept me tirelessly wading at the surface of the shallow waters of Christianity, completely missing the point of what grace is all about.

There is a reason why a discipline-based approach to the spiritual life doesn't work. It has to do with the expectations that influence us. While there are expectations that must be adhered to, the difference between living with freedom or not depends on who bears the burden of those expectations. When we live under the influence of obligation, we bear the burden of the duty to carry out those noble tasks.

However, there is a better way (Heb. 7:22). It is a covenant that assumes we have nothing to offer and that there is no need for an offer. God provided a new way that removes the need to fulfill our sense of duty and replaces it with the ever-present influence of *his* devotion to our spiritual well-being. Did you catch that? We assume that God's devotion to us is dependent on our devotion to him. His devotion to us will never depend on our impetuous, inconsistent, floundering devotion to him. The pauper will never have anything to offer the king who has everything he needs at his disposal for our well-being.

This chapter presents two influences on the freedom we experience in this Christian life. Paul referred to them when he wrote, "For sin shall no longer be your master, because *you are not under the law, but under grace*" (emphasis added) (Rom. 6:14). One way—the law—presents the influence where people impose expectations on themselves. Those of us who like rules—the bones of the law—tend toward performing for God. The rules we try to follow eventually translate to self-imposed expectations that often become the culprits of our misguided decisions and inconsistent devotion. The more rules we try to follow, the more rules there are for us to break. Rule-making will always lead to rule-breaking. And it is rule-breaking that perpetuates the cycle of failure and shame of the performance mindset (Col. 2:20–23).

The other way—grace—reflects an influence that comes not from our own efforts but rather from what God has done for us. He intends for us to enjoy our lives by living in peace with him, others, and ourselves (Matt. 22:37–38). These two influences stand in stark contrast to one another to accomplish that end. One way reflects the perfect law of God that exposes our imperfections yet rarely leads to real change. The other way reveals a new way for performance-minded people to relate to God. Understanding the difference between the two can lead us away from our overreliance on behaviors and disciplines and toward the influence of a better way called grace.

Life Under the Influence of the Law

Of the two influences, the law represents the one that acts as the invisible snare that entraps the unwary fly in the spider's web.

The law is what we are naturally prone toward, trapping us in a pattern of self-inflicted wounds. Following the law requires our control and activity to fulfill it, although we're never able to do so. Living "under the law" is most akin to the performance mindset (Rom. 6:14). It prompts us to obsess over our quality of life and leads us to constant change to meet our self-imposed expectations. To live under the influence of the law means, in its most basic form, living with a feeling of stringent obligation to do the right things or make the right choices that we believe are required by God to please him.

In Paul's day, it was the act of circumcision that many believed was the sign of spiritual devotion (Acts 15:1–2, Gal. 5:2–4). Paul reminded the Galatian believers that if they relied on circumcision to find freedom in Christ, they would be "obligated to obey the whole law" (Gal. 5:3). The performance mindset leads us to a similar situation. I learned this the hard way. To fulfill my obligations to God, I held regular quiet times, engaged in various spiritual disciplines, and sought recognition for a successful ministry. Guilt often followed when I failed to maintain one of these obligations. Because the law of God requires perfect obedience (Heb. 7:19), I was painfully aware of how far short I fell from that mark. Trying to do the right things or make the right decisions never actually brought the peace and rest in Christ I had hoped for. Self-effort and performance only spurred me to strive more and baited me to rehearse my failures again and again. Unmet obligations almost always overshadowed the elusive dream of freedom in Christ that Paul described to the Galatian church (Gal. 5:1).

If we keep trying to do the right things to please God, we will do nothing perfectly other than fail to live up to those expectations. In essence, the perfect law of God does its job. The failure is not with the law but with our inability to live up to the expectations of the law. As Paul suggested, we make ourselves lawbreakers by the very act of trying to do the right things but never actually being liberated from the wrong things (Gal. 2:18). We imagine that liberation happens through more effort. The more we explore grace, the less we will think about what we do, and the better off we'll be. The obligations we feel will compel us to always do more to find forgiveness or acceptance. The law does remind us of our need for forgiveness, but it leaves us desperately trying to satisfy that need by our own performance, with failure as the mark of a job poorly done.

Our entrapment in the law does not have to be the end of our story. Living under obligation to follow through on every require- ment of God is not an easy journey, so it requires our complete dependence on the grace of God. Those of us who are driven by obligation usually don't handle trust and dependence well. So God has to insert himself into our stories to turn us toward grace.

We have often heard these verses: "For it is by grace you have been saved, through faith—and this is not from yourselves, it is the gift of God—not by works, so that no one can boast" (Eph. 2:8–9). They are in a chapter that begins with the before-grace life of the believers in Ephesus. They lived dead in their sins, following the way of the world at the mercy of a cunning enemy (Eph. 2:1–2). Paul reminded them of the turning point on their journey. Two important words signified their turn toward grace: "But ... God" (Eph. 2:4).

The significance of those two small words rests in the fact that God's choice was not dependent on their choices. This "but

God" moment came before they made any decisions to change. They were living dead in their sins, following the ways of the world and the ruler of this earth, gratifying their flesh and fulfilling those desires and thoughts (Eph. 2:1–3). Their "but God" moment came to them when their hearts were still in that darkened condition and their lives reflected more of the world than the character of Christ.

God does not bring those pivotal moments into our lives because we change. Those "but God" moments come when we need to change but are unable to do so without grace. Those moments could represent different events that turn our attention toward grace such as deciding to worship at a certain church of believers or experiencing a devastating circumstance. It could be encountering a moment of repentance to deal with a personal sin or having a conversation with a friend who clarifies God's work in our life.

A "but God" moment came for me years into my ministry as a pastor and preacher. Because I sought the approval of those I led, I equated God's approval with people's approval. I placed my own ambitions above God's for most of my early ministry years, setting myself up for a more difficult road after my unexpected divorce. I see those early years of self-indulgence and the years after the divorce as necessary seasons for my access to grace. In a way, the divorce became my own "but God" moment to turn me away from self-sufficiency and eventually discover the all-sufficient grace of God (2 Cor. 12:9). Living under obligation to please God will trap us in an endless cycle of failure and shame. But I have learned that our stories can continue even when we think the last word has been written. God graciously provides us with those "but God" moments to turn us toward grace.

Life Under the Influence of Grace

In his letter to the Roman believers, Paul reminded them that they now lived under *the law of grace* (Rom. 6:14). While their intentions were most likely in the right place, making good disciplines the measure of their devotion did not reflect the work of grace. And it never does for us either (Rom. 14:16–18).

I can relate to their situation. I lived with a sense of obligation to please God, so I became hyperfocused on those noble tasks that we somehow imagine will bring us closer to God. Unwarily, I experienced what Paul rhetorically asked, "Don't you know that when you offer yourselves to someone as obedient slaves, you are slaves of the one you obey?" (Rom. 6:16). Over time, I reaped the results of a performance-driven Christian lifestyle. I became enslaved to shame because no Christian discipline or standard of holiness could resolve the feelings of failure that followed me over the years.

If living under the expectations of the law constrains us into a vicious cycle of performance and failure, how does the *law of grace* free us from our enslavement? Living under grace does not mean you are not under the influence of the law. Notice that I italicized *law of grace*. I did that to note that those are not the exact words in Romans 6:14 but are clearly implied. When you enter grace (Rom. 5:2), you live under a different law that rules over you. That new law is the "law of the Spirit who gives life," setting you free from the law of sin and death (Rom. 8:2). This law reflects the new position you enjoy today in Christ. Self-critique, judgment, and condemnation often follow those who succumb to the performance mindset. But because of grace, "there is now no condemnation for those who are in Christ

Jesus" (Rom. 8:1). To live under grace means you now live under the influence of the work of Christ by whom God has chosen to relate to us from a Father's heart of favor, love, and kindness (Rom. 5:8, Col. 2:14).

There is one similarity between the law of grace and the law of God. Both influence how we think, live, feel, and make decisions. Consider for a moment how the Spirit of Christ influences the impact of grace on your life. The law of grace acts in our spiritual lives like the law of gravity influences our earthly lives. Gravity represents a force that literally keeps us grounded so "we live and move and have our being" (Acts 17:28). We don't live thinking about the influence gravity has on us, but we would notice if gravity ceased to exist. Without it, our lives would be disrupted if not destroyed. Gravity does not represent our lives, but it represents an all-important influence on us to be able to live life the way God intended.

That is what living under the influence of grace is like. Grace keeps us grounded in the reality that we only have life because the God of all grace chose to give us life to the fullest (John 10:10). Paul described this life under the influence of grace as living with "the riches of his glorious inheritance" (Eph. 1:18). Every blessing under heaven and every good and perfect gift originates from the God of all grace, or as James describes him, "the Father of the heavenly lights" (James 1:17). Like gravity, grace allows us to know life in its fullest as God originally intended (John 10:10). All the benefits of grace are ours simply by living under its influence. There are no obligations to fulfill or things that need to change first. The influence of grace represents a mindset much like the obligations of the performance mindset, but it is defined by God's favor and lovingkindness that rule how we live and move and have our being.

The influence of grace provides the way out of the obligation to check all the boxes or suppress the impending doubts when we miss a few. Its influence is not contingent on our changing or fulfilling expectations before we can access grace. Its influence does not depend on our perfection or holy achievement in the ways of God. In fact, Scripture's presentation of grace seems to present the opposite.

If you follow the Old Testament story of the human journey from law to grace, you will find hints of grace throughout, even when the law ruled the day. For example, Isaiah recorded a timeless promise for the people of God. On the heels of an indictment against an erring people who did not follow God's ways or obey his law, Isaiah declared, "But now, this is what the Lord says— he who created you, Jacob, he who formed you, Israel: 'Do not fear, for I have redeemed you; I have summoned you by name; you are mine'" (Isa. 43:1).

As often as Israel murmured, complained, and rebelled, they never lost the favor and choice of God. They ran, and he pursued. They worshiped idols, and he forgave. They were exiled, and he redeemed and restored them. Nothing they did, good or bad, ever changed God's choice to turn toward them with love and provision. In fact, I believe the Old Testament uses the relationship that Israel—his chosen people—had with God to foreshadow what it would mean for all of us—Jew and Gentile alike—to enjoy the favor of God. No amount of disobedience or sordid stories of disgrace can ever change that God chose you.

Here is one final thought to clarify the influence of grace. Our disobedience and sinfulness are not overlooked because God relates to us with grace. Grace does not mean that God just lets us off the hook. Nor does grace mean that we will not experience consequences for our sins. When we admit our failures out of obligation to keep God pleased, confession will be more like a Band-Aid to appease the intensity of our guilt. On the other hand, grace demands that we deal transparently and intentionally with the sins in our hearts through confession and repentance. But remember, even the admission of our erring ways and the rectifying of the wrongs we have done are only possible by the kindness of God (Rom. 2:4). That means we find forgiveness and acceptance when we let grace rule and when we trust how God relates to us with favor and love despite the mess we have created.

Stories of accountability to a holy law would become narratives of a "new thing" that eradicates guilt through the power of grace (Isa. 43:19). No amount of wandering, no degree of doubting, and no disposition toward rebelling can separate us from God's choice to love us (Rom. 8:38–39). The influence of grace means that even when we wallow in the pigpen, we never cease to be the sons or daughters of the Father (Luke 15:13–16). Even when we run away, God keeps waiting and anticipating the moment when we will turn back toward his grace (Luke 15:20). This new way leads us to a new door that is open for a different kind of life with a new name and new reason to live under a new law called grace.

Jesus as the Door to a Life of Freedom from Self-Effort

Until those "but God" moments turn us to the influence of grace, many of us use Scripture to justify our obligation-based view of God. We may not intend to use Scripture that way, but the demand we feel to appease a God of justice influences our handling of Scripture. Because I lived so long with such a skewed version of God, I discovered that I had done just that. For most of my life, I viewed Scripture with the same law-based mentality that produced my self-perception as a failure and my deserved judgment from God.

I have since endeavored to read the Word of God through a lens of grace. It represents a significant change that has come from living under grace's influence. My change of approach to Scripture came after I began to explore grace throughout the Word of God. Suggesting that we need to live under the influence of grace could come across as a bit trite. But I recommend examining some of the Scriptures I have included in the Final Thoughts of this book, as well as some other good grace-based books. That won't change everything all at once, but the more you consider grace from reading and thinking about it, the more its influence will loosen the grip of performance.

One scripture verse that fell victim to my law-based mutilation of the words of God is in the Gospel of Luke. Jesus told a crowd of onlookers to "Strive to enter through the narrow door. For many, I tell you, will seek to enter and will not be able" (Luke 13:24 ESV). I have always interpreted that verse with a performance-driven understanding. Strive, try, and fight to enter that narrow door, which for me meant to make the right choices. When I failed to do so, I found the broad gate that would lead to God's justifiable banishment.

My teaching as a pastor reflected that law-based understanding of the verse. I can only imagine the confusion I caused for some people. I taught that the narrow door reflected a right way of living that many will not find because they don't want to give up their wrong way of living. My belief led me to make broad judgments of those who did not live up to the ethical or moral expectations that I believed God expected of them, while I failed to seriously consider my own shortcomings.

I now understand that the narrow door Luke refers to is not an entrance that leads to right living. It points to a door that opens us to the grace of Christ and who he is as the only one we can trust with our lives (Titus 2:11). The grace of Christ is the narrow door (John 10:9, Rev. 3:20) that few of us will enter because we are naturally predisposed to trust our own efforts to please a perfect God. Self-effort actually represents the broad gate that many of us tend to find. To consider living under the influence of grace simply suggests that we now live under the influence of Christ. No longer will emotions, fears, doubts, traumas, or rejections rule our perception of God or our self-worth. By opening the door to grace, we can know who God is—the God of all grace—and experience everything he has for us as a morsel of heaven here on earth.

The perspective of the pharisaical antagonists reinforces the basis for a grace-based understanding of Luke 13:24. The religious teachers in the Gospels were the poster children of self-righteousness. Matthew implies that they were the very ones who were traveling the broad way (Matt. 5:20, 7:13–14, 23:13). It is not right living that helps us find the narrow path. If it were, the religious rulers would have been the example Jesus wanted people to follow. They were the ones the general population heralded as the epitome of righteousness.

However, Jesus presented himself as the one through whom any person can come to God, and they will find grace greeting them at the door (John 10:7). Because my history and personality predispose me to keep trying, I have concluded that if I am going to strive, I will take Jesus's direction and try to relate to him and others from the narrow door of grace. So I continue to amble along this journey, free to live loved by God—mess and all—and free to love others in their own messes, all made possible because of the influence of God's love and grace for me.

As I reflect on what all this means for my efforts over the years, I don't believe checklists are all that bad today. They keep my ADD brain focused. I certainly still adhere to a Bible-reading routine. I regularly hear the voice of God speaking quietly and intimately to my heart about any number of things. I believe the spiritual disciplines can still represent an important part of the Christian's life experience. I know this sounds contradictory to everything you just read, but I am no longer bound by the obligation to carry them out. I stay organized in prayer because there is a routine that keeps my mind focused on the voice of Christ. I read Scripture because I believe God has something to say to me today. I enjoy the quiet and solitude of moments of meditation and reflection because God has quieted my soul from the constant turmoil of activity to please him. The television is still turned on, and I have a lot to learn about this influence called grace. I have reflected on the years of failed efforts to live up to a law-based sense of obligation to please God. But I must consider this: What if grace means that my worth comes not from doing anything for God but from simply being favored by him?

CHAPTER 2

Myth: If I live a holy life and make good choices, then God will be pleased with me.

What if grace means ...

God gives you the desire to do the right thing in the first place.

We now turn our attention to the motivation behind our efforts to maintain the checklists and change our behaviors to keep God pleased. Those of us with a performance mindset are obsessed with what we do and how we do it. We believe that what we do can influence God's approval of us. Most of us would argue that no one can be saved by works. But doing the right things or making the right decisions reinforce our subconscious belief that somehow God will continue to favor us because of what we do or choose not to do.

People have asked me over the years about whether certain types of behaviors could disqualify them from God's love. Normally, the questions are not worded like that. Folks usually word their questions like a child wondering if a parent could still love them after they found out they disobeyed. As varied as the questions are, so are the issues I've been asked about. The ironic thing is that many of the same questions have plagued my own mind. However, my friends had the humility I never had. They were vulnerable enough to find the answers to their questions.

The questions we ponder regarding the imaginary red line of God's love and approval often indicate that we are more focused on what we can do for God than what he does for us. We become the center of our own universe by dwelling on how we live. We believe that if we fail to live up to God's standards (at least the ones we believe are important), then God's anger or, worse yet, disappointment cannot be appeased. To please God, we keep an accounting like a sacred ledger that catalogs our sins and tallies our acts of righteousness. We secretly hope that our good deeds will outweigh our bad on some imaginary scale of righteousness that we have concocted in our minds. We strive to keep all those rigid disciplines we discussed in the previous chapter, all in an effort to please God.

How Our Works Reflect God's Work in Us

Our preoccupation with self-righteous works to find God's approval is rooted in pride. For people who struggle with shame, self-preoccupation manifests differently than those who believe they are superior to others. The guilt-ridden person rarely thinks of themselves as better than others. In fact, it is very likely that they think worse of themselves. On the other hand, the haughty person tends to think more of themselves than they should. Both perspectives—the shamed and the haughty—come from the same place: a sense of pride that results in an elevated view of self. One perspective surrenders the individual to self-condemnation. The other one results in arrogant self-righteousness. In both cases, self becomes the pinnacle of thoughts, consideration, and preoccupation.

Prioritizing grace does not mean we should lay aside the importance of what we do or how we live. While we are not saved by works (Eph. 2:8), that does not mean there are no works involved, nor does it mean that works are not important. Even Jesus declared that "the work of God is this: to believe in the one he has sent" (John 6:29). Paul provided perspective that will guide our thinking about the influence grace has on why we do what we do for God. He wrote, "Therefore, my dear friends, as you have always obeyed—not only in my presence, but now much more in my absence—continue to work out your salvation with fear and trembling, for it is God who works in you to will and to act in order to fulfill his good purpose" (Phil. 2:12–13). Although the word *grace* is never used in these verses, it is at least implied if we understand grace as God's self-initiating choice to work in us from his nature of kindness and favor, independent of our work for him.

There are a few principles in these verses that imply how God's work may influence our freedom from the effects of a performance mentality. First, notice that we and God both have a part to play in this salvation process. In response to some inquisitive questioners, Jesus indicated that even faith is considered a work of God to produce what might be considered "the works God requires" (John 6:28-29). But don't misunderstand. Grace means that God's work in us does not depend on what we do for him. Grace means that God chose us with perfect lovingkindness to do something through us despite our having no credentials, no pedigree, and no moral character to be up to the job.

The very fact that Paul wrote "to work out your salvation" indicates the amazing work of grace that God chose to work in us to produce the work through us that he requires. The part we play in this process acts as our response to the work that God is already doing in us. We don't do right things to motivate God to accept us. We do right things because God is working to enable us to do them.

Many people struggle with grace. They believe that focusing on grace relinquishes our responsibility to live right before God (Rom. 6:1). Grace does just the opposite. It demands us to be honest with ourselves and God about our preoccupation on our self-importance. Grace sets self aside by elevating the importance of God's initiative to heal what is broken in us (Rom. 6:6). Broken people cannot heal their own brokenness. It takes the love and kindness of God to heal our hard hearts caused by our own self-inflicted wounds and the choices of broken people around us. The part we play in the works we do for God represents our response to his work first being done in us. That starts with acknowledging how messed up we are and how selfish we have been in spite of God's first choice to accept us in an unacceptable condition.

While we respond to God's work through our own, the works we do occur within the context of what Paul calls "fear and trembling." That important phrase provides a clue to understand the full backdrop of grace's influence on what we do for God. I realized several years ago how much pride played a part in my performance mindset. It is not that I didn't love God, but it was that I loved God so much that I felt unworthy for God to love me back. I had it backward. I did not comprehend that God is not obligated to love me back as a response to my noble efforts. He already decided to love me before I ever chose to love him in return (1 John 4:19). God is teaching me many years later to embrace that I am already and always have been loved. It is by embracing that truth that I am being set free from adhering to a law-based performance mindset so I can enjoy life under the influence of grace.

However, if I had understood earlier what Paul meant by working out my salvation with fear and trembling, my story could have been different. When Paul wrote "fear and trembling" in Philippians 2:12, he did not mean fear as reflected by manic phobia or trembling as the result of that fear. Paul used fear and trembling to shift our perspective from what we do to why God alone is worthy of all we can do for him. To do his work with fear and trembling takes a great degree of humility that produces a dependence on God to do his work in us without thinking that there is something we need to do for him.

Anytime we place a great importance on what we do, we are placing ourselves above God (James 4:6). That is why Jesus said that true disciples will deny themselves by putting self-importance to death (Mark 8:34). Rather than placing importance on our self-effort, which is a product of pride, we must do what we do from a complete dependence on God, inspired by our reverential awe of who he is. That means I must dethrone what I do as all-important by enthroning what God is doing in me.

But dethroning self-importance is impossible without humility. We will never truly depend on God to help us become what we cannot be apart from him unless we have humility. We see this principle displayed in the life of Jesus who "did not consider equality with God something to be used to his own advantage" (Phil. 2:6). When Jesus became a man, he did so with the full understanding of who he was as God. He did not neglect himself by denying who he was but rather emptied himself of his own importance to complete the Father's redemptive plan for humanity through him.

The influence of God's grace does not mean we must neglect what we need or who we are. It means we surrender to him as he gives us what only he can give us and makes us only who he can make us be. When Jesus called Simon and Andrew to follow him to an important work, he said, "Follow me, and I will make you fishers of men" (Matt. 4:19 ESV). Notice the words Jesus used: "I will make you." Simon and Andrew did not have to follow a formula or attend a course. They did not have to accumulate notches in their belts to be known as fishers of people. The work of God in them would produce what was necessary for them to do his work. Their new identity was a product of God's work to make them who they could not be on their own.

Surely we might say that the work of God required something from them. When Peter reflected on that moment later in his life, he concluded just the opposite—that following the Lord's example required entrusting himself to the Savior even as Jesus entrusted himself to the Father (1 Pet. 2:23). As an older man, Peter knew what it took to be able to fish for people, to deliver himself over to the work of God who made him someone he could not be apart from the influence of God's work in him. Peter had to depend on his master, Jesus, much like Jesus depended on his Father's work to complete his own. It was Jesus who remarked, "I tell you, the Son can do nothing by himself. He does only what he sees the Father doing. Whatever the Father does, the Son also does" (John 5:19). What was required of Peter was to deliver himself over to the work of his master to do in him what could not be done without him, much like Jesus submitted to the work of his Father to accomplish his own redemptive plan for humanity.

It takes humility to entrust yourself to God like those first disciples. Even though humility means we take a modest view of ourselves, neglecting ourselves does not mean we are humble, as Paul indicated to another group of people (Col. 2:23). The work of grace precludes that we regard God and others before ourselves, leading us to a place of humble service (Phil. 2:7–8). We depend on God's work in us to do the works we accomplish for him. Our works accomplish what Paul calls the completion of our salvation (Phil. 1:6, 2:12).

How God's Work in Us Produces His Work Through Us

Now let's focus on Philippians 2:13: "For it is God who works in you *to will* and *to act* in order to fulfill his good purpose" (emphasis added). The two italicized phrases demonstrate how grace influences what we do for God and why we do it. It took me a while, but eventually I learned that my life in Christ is not about me; it's about him. Sometimes that lesson takes a long time to learn, as I discovered. God's activity in our lives to produce our willingness to act shows how it is virtually impossible to claim that our work is a product of our initiative apart from God's initiative to accomplish what he decided long ago to do in us and through us.

God works in us at the two most basic levels of human nature—to will and to act—and both of them influence human behavior. These two human traits originate from God's original work of grace in our lives. They relate to our desire to please God and the steps we take to follow through on those motivations. As an educator, I tell students all the time that it is never good enough to simply set a goal if you don't intend to follow through on that goal. God's work occurs at these two most basic levels of human motivation and effort to do what he calls us to do and be who he makes us to be.

First, consider what it means to desire God as our motivation to do what we do for God. Paul uses the word *will* to indicate our desire to do our work for God. The word "will" (Greek: *thelo*) has a range of meanings in Greek that include intention and volition. It indicates that our desire for God is not just an empty wish or a thought we tritely possess, but rather an intentional focus that leads to a decisive action. In other words, Paul indicates by using the word *thelo* that those in whom God does his work will follow through with intentionality to accomplish his work through them. That's good news for those of us trapped by performance.

There is virtue in our desire to please God. Most of us have a résumé of activity for God. We can recount not only how we may have failed God but remember, if we think hard enough, the things we have done for God. Philippians 2:13 means that the desires we possess for God and the activities they produce originate from God, not from ourselves. At some point, though, our law-based performance mindset influenced our desires to become unbridled from the gracious work of God to put that desire for him within us.

I argue that without God giving us a desire for him, it would be virtually impossible to even attempt something on his behalf, whether it's a question in the heart of a desperate follower or the sermon notes of a broken and misguided preacher. For performance-minded people, there is an intensity to our madness. We strive, we work, and we guilt and shame ourselves when we don't measure up, all for the idea that we might be found pleasing in the eyes of God.

The psalmist captures the intensity of this desire. "As the deer pants for streams of water, so my soul pants for you, my God" (Ps. 42:1). The Hebrew word for *pant* is the equivalent of a Greek word that means "to yearn or earnestly desire." Like a desert wanderer whose parched mouth longs for that precious drop of water, the person with a deep longing for God will follow through with the intentionality of a dehydrated and dying wanderer at every good and bad turn of life. If someone is truly thirsty, there is nothing else that can capture imagination or attention. Every intent and every desire is to find that source of life.

I understand what the psalmist meant by such an intense kind of desire amidst the twists and turns of my own sordid tale. I blamed myself for the many years of conflict my family had to endure after the divorce. However, as grace influenced me to consider the wounds and faults that shaped how I responded to that painful time, I found I could relate to that deer panting for water to survive. The deepest longing of my heart was to serve God in the original way I understood his call. However, my damaged pride from failing to please God overshadowed my desire to serve him.

Discouragement caused my aimless wandering and despondent questioning for several years. But grace kept pointing me back to the water. I sensed my longing for God amidst my anger and doubts. The longing itself reflected the intensity of my desire that could only be present because of God's work in me. Like many of my friends who pondered the questions that lingered from the memories of their own faults, the questions themselves spoke louder than the innuendos of failure we rehearsed in our minds. Our God-ordained desire for him prompts our curiosity to question, negating the doubts that plagued our hearts.

We see the failures. We relive the divorces. We lament the fateful decisions that carved a broken path forward. But our desire for God that prompts our inquiries reflects one who perseveres with a longing that is deeply embedded in our hearts by the God who never gives up on the wandering one searching for the precious waters of grace. As the Good Shepherd leads us, often outside our own awareness, we find all we want as he gently guides us to rest in the green pastures of his faithfulness and steadfast love (Ps. 23:1). It is our desire for the waters of grace that explain our striving, and it is God's first work in us to produce that desire for him that keeps us following him there.

If it is true that God puts an intense desire within us for him, then why do our desires continue to go awry? Paul lamented this very fact. "For I know that good itself does not dwell in me, that is, in my sinful nature. For I have the *desire* to do what is good, but I cannot carry it out" (emphasis added) (Rom. 7:18).

Paul uses the same word here for *desire* as he laments his own regrets that he used in his letter to the church at Philippi (Phil. 2:13). Isn't this the story of our lives? Apparently, we are in good company. We have the intense desire to do good, but it is impossible to carry it out if left to ourselves. And that is the answer to what makes our desires go astray. We go wrong when we are left to ourselves, causing our desires to fall prey to a selfish heart. That is because godly living, or however you want to label it, will always become about us when we separate the truth of our brokenness from the unmerited grace of God.

For Paul, it may have been about him at some point as a Jew fulfilling the legal and moral responsibilities of God's law (Rom. 7:25). For me, my desire was about being recognized by others because I felt God's approval when I heard others' approval. Anytime I perceived that someone had rejected me or ignored the good job I had done, I subconsciously believed that God had rejected me. I failed to understand that what I did or didn't do was driven by an intense desire that God himself had planted within me. While our desire to perform reflects good intentions gone astray, without God's original work of grace to produce the desire in us, we would have never wanted to please him in the first place.

Now let's shift our attention to the motivation behind our desire for God. Look again at Philippians 2:13 (ESV): "For it is God who works in you, both to will and *to work* for his good pleasure" (emphasis added). We get our word *energy* from this word for "work" (Greek: *energeo*). It's as if Paul describes how God's work of grace in us produces our desire for him that in turn results in the energy we have to follow through on the work we do for God.

Again, our work for God could never happen without the influence of grace. God plants a seed of desire by choosing to use the circumstances of life that draw us to him (John 6:44). God draws us at the moment of salvation (John 6:37) and continually draws us as we work out our salvation. But in many cases, it is a seed of desire that goes dormant for many years, resulting in a works mindset without ever considering the God-placed desire that's buried underneath a lot of misguided activity. A dormant seed of desire could occur for any number of reasons—trauma, family pain, loss, inaccurate understanding of God. For me, the influence of religious legalism and a personality prone toward activity produced a mindset that led to decades of cyclical failure. The more I worked to carry out what God had called me to do, the more I found it never satisfied that deep longing in my heart to please God. I struggled with remembering every sin I had committed. I tried to position my life to avoid sin, which never worked because it seemed the more I did, the more conscious I became of sin. That is exactly what Paul described about his own experience (Rom. 3:20).

It took a long time to interpret my misguided activity as a work of God to produce the energy—the conditions for growth—to continue the search for peace with God and peace in my heart. Eventually, the water of the word of grace (Acts 20:32, Eph. 5:26) reached that dormant seedling that then emerged from its hardened shell, produced by inadequate conditions for growth. When the word of grace penetrated my hardened heart, I found the inspiration to strive for that narrow door that led me to the grace of a Savior I so deeply sought to please, opening me to a whole new life with him.

The energy we put into what we do for God manifests as we follow through on what we desire to do for him. Just as the desire to find the water of life comes from God himself, so the energy we use to follow through on that desire can come from no other source than the one who gave us the desire in the first place. His grace reflects his choice to plant those seedlings of desire that emerge along the broken paths of our lives, leading us to follow him to the green pastures of his steadfast love.

The Work That Gives God Pleasure

Imagine this. Paul says our desire to work for him and the energy we put into fulfilling that work *brings God pleasure* (Phil. 2:13 ESV). Because grace never means the absence of works, it is precisely through what we do that pleases God. Our labor for God can never be separate from the work he does in us to produce our desire to serve him. From an ancient promise God gave his people, he admonished them to never let their "hands grow weak. The Lord your God is in your midst, a mighty one who will save; he will rejoice over you with gladness; he will quiet you by his love; he will exult over you with loud singing" (Zeph. 3:16–17 ESV).

The writer reminded Israel that God never desires that we quit working or that our hands grow weak. Paul picked up this theme when he wrote, "Never tire of doing what is good" (2 Thess. 3:13). The desire you feel to do for God may be based on a misconceived idea of what God requires. But don't be mistaken. God does not advocate for us to give up doing good. He simply calls us to find our rest in the good work he is doing in us to produce the work he will accomplish through us each day.

Both the journey of activity to do what he enables us to do and the work he does through us each day are what bring God pleasure. Our desire to please God by what we do is not borne from our own initiative. God gave us that desire, and he has enabled us to act on that desire with the works we do. The problem is not inherent within the activity. The problem is that we trust the activity to make us pleasing to God when our desperate desire to please our Father is what alone brings him pleasure.

Today, favor feels completely different than the obligation I felt all those years ago. I have accepted my story for all of its good and bad effects on my life. "For by the grace of God I am what I am, and his grace to me was not without effect. No, I worked harder than all of them—yet not I, but the grace of God that was with me" (1 Cor. 15:10). I had worked hard to please God through developing personal devotion and succeeding in ministry. And then when divorce loomed over me like a dark cloud, I discovered that this season was a "but God" moment that would take many years for me to comprehend. It was then that I finally saw the smile I had longed to put on God's face for many years, only made possible by his favor and kindness shining on me in this very dark season. It reminded me of that ancient blessing that God gave his people: "May the Lord bless you and protect you. May the Lord smile on you and be gracious to you. May the Lord show you his favor and give you his peace" (Num. 6:24–26 NLT).

It was the kindness of God that never quit watering the seeds of desire within me with the word of grace. The desire to please him that produced so many fruitless works and the ledger that somehow was always found wanting would be the very seedlings that emerged from my darkest days of brokenness. As misguided as our efforts may be, think about this: What if grace means that God finds pleasure in what we do because he gave us the desire to please him in the first place with the intensity of a person thirsting to be loved by God?

CHAPTER 3

Myth: If I have a messy life, then God will not choose or accept me.

What if grace means ...

God chooses you just as you are, mess and all.

It could be argued that our stories are the sum of the decisions we've made in our lives. It's almost as if we think our decisions are the most important part of our relationship with God because they determine what he decides to do with us. As much as we lament many of the choices we've made, those with a performance mindset will find that grace puts our decisions in their proper place. This chapter will show how our overemphasis on our choices is reversed by the gracious choice of God to love us despite the sum of our decisions.

As I reflected on those signature moments of my story, I found that I have made some good decisions and some bad ones. While that could be left unsaid, if you knew my self-perception as a Christian with a failed performance mindset, you would assume that the bad decisions far outweighed the good ones. Even when I was enjoying success in ministry, I rehearsed past moments of failure, which made me feel unqualified to do what he had called me to do. I privately hoped that God did not regard my mistakes as much as he regarded my desire to honor him with a life well-lived. Most of the time, I did not believe I was living the kind of life God wanted from me. I thought of God holding an impossible, cosmic measuring stick ready to hang that carrot of perfection in front of me, even though I would probably never taste its sweet nectar.

But then grace entered the story. Grace rewrote my story of self-reliance and performance by shifting my attention from my condemning self to the gracious and loving God who "keeps no record of wrongs" (1 Cor. 13:5). Being the God of all grace, he chose to relate to us with kindness and favor, with no recollection of our past mistakes (Mic. 7:18–19). I lived most of my life as a believer and pastor, privately thinking that God was my judge who was poised to levy judgment for all the bad decisions of my life. I have discovered, though, that grace is not a decision by which I must convince God to reward my choices. I have learned that the choice of God to regard me with grace has always been his plan and is simply who he is.

It Is God's Design and Nature to Choose Us

God's graciousness and mercy reflect his design for how he has chosen to relate to us as the perfect Father and the nature of who he is as God. Of all the ways Scripture describes how God chose to relate to us—friend/friend, Lord/servant, teacher/student—grace best reflects his plan to relate to us as a parent to a child.

It is the Father/son/daughter relationship that best explains the favor of God's gracious choice.

Paul wrote that God "predestined us for *adoption to sonship* through Jesus Christ, in accordance with his pleasure and will—to the praise of his glorious grace" (emphasis added) (Eph. 1:5–6). Those verses mean that grace reflects all the permanence and unconditional love that exist between a father and a child. It is from the context of that type of relationship that God chooses to love us. If you struggle with thinking of God as a father because of your own childhood experiences, then think of God as you would think of your own children. We try to protect our children; we comfort them when they hurt; we guide them when they have lost their way. Nothing can change our position with God as his children even as nothing can change the position of my own children to me as their father.

Jesus suggested to a confused, religious teacher that we are born from above much like we are born on earth (John 1:12–13, 3:3–5). When we experience the new birth into God's family, the Father adopts us and sees us as co-heirs with his Son and—don't miss it—heirs of the Father too (Rom. 8:14–17). As children of God, we have all that God has and all that God promises in Christ. You are his, and nothing can change that. The Father sees you in the same manner as he sees Jesus, his Son. Legally, you have been adopted into this royal, divine family with all the promises of a family member by birth.

But beyond what it means to be adopted, the Father sees you as if the blood of his Son courses through your veins. Even if a father chose to disown his own children, nothing could ever change that they are still his children by blood, even though he may never utter their name again. Those of us who are born from above are born anew by the blood of Christ (John 3:3, Heb. 9:22, Eph. 2:13, 1 Pet. 1:18–19). When we are born into his family, grace means that God can never forsake us any more than a loving, responsible parent can forsake their own (Ps. 103:13, Isa. 54:10, 2 Tim. 2:13, Heb. 13:5).

While grace has always reflected the Father's choice, God chooses us also because it is simply his nature to give us grace when we don't deserve it. When Moses met with God on one occasion, God described himself to the leader of Israel as "the compassionate and gracious God" (Exod. 34:6). God used two words—Hebrew: *rachuwm* and *channuwn*—to describe himself to his people as one who feels compassionate mercy and a sense of favor. His mercy is deep-seated within his very being, and his graciousness speaks of his predisposition to never forsake his people. It is no wonder that he continued to choose for the good of his people when they gave him every reason to walk away. His own description of himself reflects his nature to relate to his people with favor and mercy.

His merciful and gracious nature is seen on a number of occasions in the Old Testament (2 Chron. 30:9, Neh. 9:17, Ps. 103:8). Israel's past demonstrated continual rebellion against God's plan (Deut. 32:5–6), but the favor of God followed them no matter how far they strayed (Deut. 32:10–12, Jer. 31:1–2). He never relented from relating to them with a father's heart that could never abandon them but always extended mercy to give what they never deserved (Exod. 4:22–23, Deut. 1:31). To do anything differently would have contradicted who he is as God (Ps. 103:8, Joel 2:13).

We who follow Christ have inherited the same favor that motivated God to always find a way to draw Israel back to himself when they offered him no reason to do so. The nature of God to favor us from a heart of kindness will always mean he is predisposed to love us when we are unlovable, wait on us when we chart our own paths, bless us when we don't deserve it, pursue us when we are on the run, choose us when we don't qualify, declare us righteous when we are not, and protect us when we are at our weakest (Ps. 5:12, Luke 15:20, Rom. 5:19, 2 Cor. 5:21, Eph. 1:3, 1 John 3:1). Grace reflects his predisposition to choose us, and that choice has always been his plan.

Grace and the Choices That God and We Make

Our Father chooses to relate to us by grace because that is who he is. But grace also has everything to do with the choices God and we make. When we speak of grace, it relates to God's decisions on our behalf and how our choices relate to his. We find just such an understanding in a letter the Apostle Paul wrote. Romans 11:5–6 (NASB 1995) describes grace this way: "In the same way then, there has also come to be at the present time a remnant according to *God's gracious choice*. But *if it is by grace, it is no longer on the basis of works*, otherwise *grace is no longer grace*" (emphasis added).

Consider the three phrases in italics. First, grace reflects "*God's gracious choice*." God's relationship with his people has always been defined by grace. It is hard to admit sometimes, but those of us with a performance mindset elevate the importance of our decisions because we believe our desire to be the people God wants us to be will somehow convince him to be more pleased with us. Because we believe that what we do is all-important, we dismiss notions that God chose to work in us before we chose to work for him. If you struggle with that idea, I imagine that you wrestled through the last chapter. I get the struggle. There are many aspects of my grace story that I am still struggling with.

The struggle for many of us comes from controlling the if-then relationship with God that we have concocted. If I do A, then B will happen. If I choose to live a holy life, then God will choose to love me. If I choose to quit this habit, then God will choose to forgive me. We become the puppeteer in this scenario who pulls God's strings by trying to influence how he responds to our best intentions of self-effort. We do this to calm our anxiety and reduce our guilt, but often to no avail. We still imagine that controlling our relationship with God will make us feel better until we realize that we are limited by our inability to control ourselves. Eventually, we may discover that God's choice had nothing to do with our getting the first half of the if-then equation right. He chose us, fully knowing that we would never hold up our side of the deal.

Grace also means that God's decision to choose us is more important than our decisions for him. Paul said that *"if it is by grace, it is no longer on the basis of works"* (emphasis added) (Rom. 11:6 NASB 1995). God's choices are not influenced by our choices. Our good decisions do nothing to convince God to love us more, nor do our bad decisions convince him to favor us less. Whether we realize it or not, our efforts are simply our response to his love and kindness toward us. He chose to love us when we were still unlovable. Everything we have and everything we do comes from the overflow of his choice to first love us (1 John 4:19). When we struggle to love him and others, we can be sure that we are being influenced by some form of obligation to love because we lack the capacity to love like him without living from within his choice to love us first.

Jesus said, "As I have loved you, so you must love one another" (John 13:34). Here is the problem with our ability to love like him. We are naturally bent toward choosing our own way. While God's nature is to choose for our good, our selfish nature is to make choices from our selfish desires. Self-obsession sabotages our relationship with God and others. We live in this reality every day because Adam and Eve first took this path (Rom. 5:18). God told them they could eat from any tree except the tree of the knowledge of good and evil (Gen. 2:16–17). Even though God defined his choice, we find Adam and Eve a short time later choosing to eat of the fruit anyway. The snake lured Eve with the fruit that was pleasing to her eye. The bait was set, she looked, and they both chose to eat (Gen. 3:6).

But take heart! Adam and Eve continued in favor with God even after the fall. That was evidenced by God clothing them with garments of skin for redemption to cover the shame of their sin (Gen. 3:21) and producing a lineage that would ultimately lead to the ancestry of the promised Messiah (Luke 3). God's gracious choice is unthwarted by our definable moments of failure. God chooses to love us, and there is nothing dumb enough that we could do to change that. The decisions we make to prove our love for God or the ones that indict us for loving something else more than him can never change his choice to love us first.

Finally, our preoccupation with self can nullify grace, which means that *"grace is no longer grace."* There is a point when grace loses the uniqueness of God's choice. That point is when we interject our efforts, our solutions, or our choices. It is then that grace no longer looks like grace. We muddle the kindness of God when we blaze our own paths outside the influence of the provision and goodness of God.

You may think, then, that grace may nullify the importance of our choices. Actually, grace reinforces the importance of our choices. It is entirely true that grace reflects God's gracious choice, and it is equally true that we who are created in the image of God can choose. Our choices occur in what I call that sweet spot where God's favor works itself out through our lives. We experience the sweet spot of life when we make our decisions about life under the influence of grace.

The story of Adam and Eve illustrates this point. God did not limit their choices in the Garden of Eden. He defined their choices within the Garden he provided for them. They had the capacity for good and bad decisions as they lived under the influence of God's grace toward them. God placed them in the Garden that was lavishly suited for all their needs. Their choices were infinite within the boundary of that gracious gift, even if it meant they had the capacity to make choices outside his will. That means grace will never look like grace, nor will we ever feel favored when we choose outside of God's favor in our lives. When we choose outside of grace, we are prone to depend on ourselves to have what God never intended or to fix something in our lives we could never fix. Grace does not limit the importance of our decisions; grace puts context on them within that sweet spot of life where we enjoy God's gracious provisions.

Grace has everything to do with the choices that God and we make. But remember, our choices can no more influence God to love us more or less than the misbehavior of a toddler in a grocery store can lessen the love of a parent for their child. Grace means that God chooses to relate to us without regard to our worst performance or the best of what we could offer him. The choice of God to relate to us by grace was best seen when the Father sent his Son for a fallen world as the ultimate expression of love for those who least deserve it.

The Grace of Christ and the Truth of Our Brokenness

God demonstrated his love for us by choosing to send Jesus to bear the guilt of every bad decision we have made. John wrote, "We have seen his glory, the glory of the one and only Son, who came from the Father, *full of grace and truth*" (emphasis added) (John 1:14). To fully understand God's disposition to choose us when we are predisposed to choose outside his will depends on understanding grace in the context of truth.

Grace relates to what God chose to do on our behalf, while truth enables us to trust God for his mercy, despite our bad decisions. Resting in the grace of God is not possible without truth. When we separate truth from grace it can become more propositional than personal, reflecting the shifting sands of self-reliance and the volatility of the emotions that follow. Most of the time we relegate truth to an abstract idea that relates to some notion we feel the need to speak up about or a belief we need to hold. The problem with that limited understanding of truth is that it can lead to what my pastor calls "moralistic Christianity." When truth reflects what we believe or how we live, it is easy to fall into the trap of trusting a moral compass based on right living or right believing. Truth in this context is still based on what we do or how we think.

A deeper understanding of truth will always point us back to what God does by grace. The word for truth (Greek: *aletheia*) can be traced back to two Hebrew words—*emeth* (certainty, faithfulness) and *emunah* (faithfulness, steadfastness)—that point to the certainty and faithfulness of God's decision to relate to us by grace. The truth of God's grace means we can trust what he says. To say that his "word is truth" (John 17:17) is to say that his word is certain and sure to be what he says it is to be. What God says is what he does. He said before the beginning of time that he would relate to his people by grace. If we continue in that word, the truth of grace will set us free (John 8:31–32).

There are two examples when these Hebrew words were used to point to the assurance that a promise made is a promise kept. Rahab the prostitute pled for the safety of her family when Israelite spies scouted the city of Jericho. The spies assured her, "If you don't tell what we are doing, we will treat you kindly and faithfully [Hebrew: *emeth*] when the Lord gives us the land" (Josh. 2:14). This woman would have understood that the spies were assuring her of the certainty of their commitment to keep the promise they had just made. On another occasion, Jeremiah suggested that God's faithfulness (Hebrew: *emunah*) is as sure as the sun rising in the morning for those of us who deserve it the least (Lam. 3:22–23). To relate to us in any other way than grace, despite our extreme brokenness, would be no more possible than disrupting the certainty of the morning dawn. When Jesus came to earth, he perfectly embodied the absolute nature of the grace of God to love the unlovable and gave us the assurance to trust that he will only relate to us from that place.

The performance mindset, however, creates doubts in our minds and uncertainty in our hearts. The truth of grace makes doubt disappear, and the uncertainty of our decisions bows to the assurance of his grace. Doubts can cause us to think that if we were God, we would never choose us. But because of God's nature, which is perfectly embodied in the person of Jesus, he always chooses the imperfect, the lowly, and the insignificant. Because God relates to us from grace and truth, he knows our desperate need for him, so he offers "the incomparable riches of his grace, expressed in the kindness to us in Jesus Christ" (Eph. 2:7).

Though God never overlooks our brokenness, he always deals with our human frailty because grace would have no meaning if God chose to overlook our lost nature. Just as he will always choose to clothe the purity of divinity with the imperfect flesh of humanity, the reality of grace is this: God decided a long time ago to choose people we would never choose. It's not that we would be chosen last for his team. It's that we would always be left waiting to be chosen because we will never have what it takes to be on his team because of a lifetime of bad decisions. The graciousness of God's nature and the certainty of his promise means that God's gracious choice has always been and will always be for the imperfect you.

I privately doubted this truth for most of my life. I wondered how this could be. If I hit the rewind button on my life, I could think of all the choices I made that reflected my prideful self-sufficiency, disqualifying me from ever being chosen. Then I revisited these verses: "If God is for us, who can be against us? He who did not spare his own Son, but gave him up for us all—how will he not also, along with him, graciously give us all things?" (Rom. 8:31–32). The more I read it the more I believed it. God's choice for us was not based on our goodness but rather on the fact that he did not spare his only Son. He chose to forsake his Son on our behalf and therefore chooses to freely give us all the benefits of his choice. The truth of who we are as ones prone to mask our bad decisions or think more highly of ourselves than we ought does not disqualify us from God's favor. If our broken nature did disqualify us from his decision to love us, then the narrative of the Gospels would never include the scores of encounters the perfect Son of God had with very imperfect, banished people.

God's Choice and Our Self-Perception

Our natural tendency is to make decisions that look more like our fallen nature than the perfect nature of God. Our need to relive the past causes a predisposition to self-reliance. The worse we feel, the more inclined we are to fix ourselves. Grace will always reveal the enormity of God's love when we've given him no reason to love us. This is so because he sees us in Christ before we have become Christ-like.

The performance mindset does just the opposite. Our effort to change the decisions we have made in life, which our history continues to tell us we cannot change, only reinforces a self-perception of faults and failures. God chose us by grace in our state of brokenness. God will always choose us when we still have problems to fix (Rom. 5:8). Even when we are still prone to bad decisions, a poor self-perception, or an insatiable need to perform for God's approval, his love and kindness provide us with a new position in his sight. We are now the chosen of God, already declared holy and already accepted as the beloved (Col. 3:12). He did not mandate us to change a habit or belief before he would choose us any more than Jesus required Paul to change his blaspheming, persecuting ways before he met the Messiah on the road to Damascus (Acts 9:1–4, 1 Tim. 1:12–16). His choice for us does not depend on our efforts, good decisions, or moral progress. Love motivated the Father to choose us, fully knowing that our choices would look more like the rebellious heart of a child than the perfect holiness of God.

At times you may feel like the woman at the well in an endless chain of hopeless relationships (John 4). But then Grace approaches you in your state of shame and repudiated isolation, giving you a new story for everyone to hear, including all those who tritely patted you on the head as a hopeless case of mental and moral impurity.

You may feel like the banished tax collector shamelessly climbing a tree to catch a glimpse of Grace walking down a dusty street, not knowing it will be your house tonight where he chooses to dine (Luke 19).

You may seem more like the rough, cussing fisherman who can't seem to catch a break or a fish. Grace steps into your boat, changing the very course of your life, not to mention your success on the lake (Matt. 4, Luke 5:1–11).

Or you may resemble the harlot with a reputation that precedes you, who just longs to wash the feet of Grace with your tears (Luke 7). You find yourself in the presence of religious scholars whose knowledge is only surpassed by their legal and moral purity. But you discover how Grace welcomes the banished, forgives the unforgivable, and silences the critics who would rather hear of someone's failure than celebrate God's love for the forgiven.

Grace always chooses first and then changes later. What if grace means that God chose you just as you are, mess and all? That would change everything, would it not?

CHAPTER 4

*Myth: If I clean up my act first, then God can use
me in his kingdom.*

What if grace means ...

*God uses you at your worst to bring out the best
for others.*

Grace makes what we do for God possible. In this chapter, we will explore the connection between grace and the service we do for God. This chapter took me the most time to write, and it was the most difficult to communicate. While I know that our acts of service are performed in direct proportion to the faith we have received (Rom. 12:6), I found that I still struggled to communicate this idea. That could be because it is impossible to convey something I have not personally realized first.

Having graduated from seminary with academic honors and preaching in churches for years, I thought I could adequately explain something so fundamental as how ministry is accomplished through us. I believed I could surely inspire all who read this book with my knowledge, experience, and creative writing. But therein lies the reason this chapter has proven to be the most difficult. I have yet to learn the vital lesson that reflects the results of grace rather than the fruit of my labor. I bring nothing to the table. I have nothing to offer except brokenness, guilt, failure, and bitterness. And it is precisely because of my utter dependence on the grace of God that I am worth anything to anyone.

It has proven to be nearly impossible for me to break the performance mindset from how and why I serve in the kingdom of God. If you can identify with my struggle, maybe you will admit with me that at times when we strive to please God through how we serve, we tend to focus on how the results of our acts of service impact us. We may expect recognition, a job-well-done accolade, a feeling of accomplishment, or a simple thank you. I had those goals, and ministry became about what I had done or my motive behind serving. We don't consciously admit that, nor would we agree in the moment that our act of service is more about us than who we are serving. But self-preoccupation is the cross that performance-driven people bear.

Sometimes the turns of life leave us grossly aware of our tendency to take the credit for what God is doing. Then life's circumstances present opportunities to be involved in something that could never be done except for the grace of God. Shortly after my divorce, I left the ministry for a new step in life. I was not sure the direction life would take me. However, I ended up serving children with disabilities in a public school. I remember when I was first interviewed for the position. I was tired, worn, and not in the best frame of mind from the wearisome effects of the divorce.

A school administrator who interviewed me was more interested than I was about a new position. When she asked me what I thought about becoming a special education teacher, I told her I knew nothing about special education and that I was not going to try to convince her that I did. She responded with the most remarkable statement that will follow me the rest of my life. She said, "You may not know anything about special education, but you know something that my teachers do not know. You know how to shepherd people, and those 17 kids in that school need a shepherd, not a teacher."

That statement framed how I would serve those kids for the following years. I did not believe I had what it took to do any good for those kids, but as it turned out, that period of time became one of the most impactful seasons of my life—a time when I could see the difference God was making through me in the lives of some very promising little kids.

I didn't get the point of what God was teaching me then, but I do now. I did not have anything worthwhile to bring to those kids, and it took that very mindset to create a sense of dependence on God to forge some of the closest relationships with coworkers that rivaled what I ever had in church ministry. At the same time, God gave me the skills I lacked to serve a population of kids who needed an average teacher who just happened to be a very experienced shepherd and by nature a consistent father figure. That season required me to know there was nothing I possessed that I could bring to the table. My dependence on God to do what I did not know how to do prepared me to receive the grace God used to serve those kids and eventually heal the very real wounds of my own heart.

The Fruit of Ministry and Our Reliance on His Work of Grace

Selflessness is best experienced with uncompromising reliance on God for everything we do. It was impossible for me to depend on my skills or knowledge when I worked in that school. I knew that if this season of life would not fall apart at the seams from yet another failure, God would have to give me what I did not have in myself in order to do whatever he had me there to do.

There is fruit that comes from serving others by fully relying on God's provision. That fruit may look like kids who develop into well-grounded young people or a healthy church that shares the word of grace with one another and the community around them. More likely than not, the fruit may just look like a different person who no longer lives for Christ out of a sense of obligation but now lives under the influence of grace.

Many years ago, my parents lived on a farm where my dad planted and grew an orchard that any professional horticulturalist would be impressed with. The fruit flourished under the care of my dad's watchful eye. A meandering vine draped over a trellis that produced luscious grapes. A sprawling garden bore a variety of vegetables that perfectly completed every meal. Fruit trees yielded a harvest of apples, peaches, and apricots. All of them quickly became his pride and joy.

Jesus referred to the fruit that we bear in the context of just such an orchard. He gave his final address to the disciples in

John 15 as he prepared them for his soon departure. He taught that our life as his followers is not a life of our own. As he is connected to the Father, we as branches stay connected to him. We see fruit bud from our lives as the conditions become suitable for growth (John 15:4, James 5:7).

Those conditions will always reflect the self-initiating, timeless work of God's grace in our lives. Jesus described those suitable conditions when he taught, "You did not choose me, but I chose you and appointed you so that you might go and bear fruit—fruit that will last—and so that whatever you ask in my name the Father will give you" (John 15:16). This was a countercultural statement in that day. Typically, in first-century Judaism, the student would choose the rabbi. But for Jesus as God in the flesh, he chose his students, and the results that would last reflected his choice and not the typical choice of the disciple.

The individual with a performance mindset, though, reverses the order of Jesus's words. We believe that we must produce fruit so God will choose us. As a result, we fall prey to our reliance on how well we live or how productive we are in God's kingdom. Self-reliance causes us to forget that God chose us and set us apart to produce fruit. Self-preoccupation can also cause us to forget what it actually means to bear fruit in the first place.

For years, I equated how well I abided in Christ with my acts of service or my performance in ministry. If I was deemed successful, then I concluded it must be because I was depending on God to do his work through me. Then I began to take another look at what it might mean to be a branch connected to the vine. I found that my life as a follower of Christ is completely dependent on him as the vine, whether I believed I was successful or not. I could do nothing more to produce fruit than the tree could do under the coercion of the farmer. A farmer does not have to convince the tree to bear fruit but rather simply create the conditions for the tree to produce fruit. That is what grace does. God in his grace creates conditions in the heart that allow the fruit of righteousness to be produced (Phil. 1:11). Fruit-bearing is God's work in us and not our own. That realization removed my sense of obligation to use service and ministry as pawns to convince God to make a difference through me for his kingdom.

I also discovered that Jesus described obedience as a type of fruit that buds from being connected to him. This realization was huge for me. Even my obedience is impossible unless his life produces the fruit of obedience to him (John 15:5). By his work of grace, my obedience to do what he has appointed me to do reflects my loving response to what he has done in me as the branch who is connected to the vine (John 15:10). That gave new meaning to the idea that I could do nothing apart from him, and that included every act of obedience I would do for him. I concluded that the fruit of our labor, then, becomes less about what we do for God and more about what he does through us for the benefit of all those around us. It is a high calling to be a branch under the care of the Vinedresser, chosen and appointed to share the love of God that we have received from Christ the Vine (John 13:34–35, John 15:16, 2 Tim. 1:9).

Grace Defines Servanthood from a Sense of Brokenness

Our reliance on God's work in us to produce what he has chosen to do through us reveals our complete dependence on him. Apart from him, we are broken. Apart from him, we have no life. Apart from him, we have no potential. Without him we can do nothing (John 15:5). The nature of grace requires that we never forget that. The moment we fail to remember that apart from him we have nothing to give is the moment we fall prey to the likely failures that follow the performance mindset.

Rehearsing our dependence on God's grace liberates us from selfishly working to impress others, aspiring for recognition, or rehearsing our failures. My pastor often says that grace is remembering just how sinful we are but relishing in how great we are loved, thus realizing how hopeful we have become. He says it much better than I have written here. In any event, grace cascades over a once-barren cliff like a waterfall from the spring rains when we serve in utter dependence on God for the benefit of those around us.

A moment between Jesus and his disciples illustrates this point. After a powerplay from a few of his disciples, Jesus described how denying self is the entryway into greatness and leadership, which represent the very things many of us may aspire to (Matt. 20:25–28). He contrasted how the secular rulers of their time ruled from a place of power and authority. Instead, he taught how his followers who desire greatness in the kingdom of God should become servants to the ones they desire to wield power over. Those who may aspire to be the leader among a group must become a slave to those they hope to lead. Ultimately, his followers would give their lives away as they followed his example of self-less service. It is impossible to believe that we could interpret what we do for others in any other way than how grace flows from our lives at the convergence of self-sacrifice and the priority of those we serve.

This radical vision for serving lavished through the grace of God is counterintuitive to the performance mindset. Performance requires the consideration of self over others, pursues the recognition for a job well done, and fixates on a to-do-list model of Christianity. Serving from a place of brokenness will always put others before self. Encouragement, unity, comfort, love, compassion, and joy are all the fruits of considering others ahead of self (Phil. 2:1–4). Even when judgment could be levied against someone in a local congregation who may not deserve mercy and grace, it is precisely in that context that the law of Christ is fulfilled. We put the love of God on display for the world to recognize us as the disciples of Christ (John 13:34–35, Gal. 6:2). Think about it. Grace from ones who are completely dependent on grace themselves give grace to those who deserve no grace. That is the grace-based paradigm for service that Jesus instructed his disciples to carry out.

We Bring Nothing to the Table

Grace acts as a currency of heaven when we give something away that we ourselves do not possess apart from God's gracious gift. We receive grace to give grace away. Paul explained to the church in Ephesus that he received grace to administer grace on their behalf (Eph. 3:2). That can only happen when the one who is acting as the conduit for grace understands that we give grace from what we don't possess ourselves. We serve out of our brokenness. We love from the bottomless well of God's love. We give the mercy we have first received as dependents of his mercy. We share out of our poverty. We follow the example of our Savior by which "the grace of our Lord Jesus Christ, that though he was rich, yet for your sake he became poor, so that you through his poverty might become rich" (2 Cor. 8:9). He emptied himself to become a servant of God so we could become what we could never be apart from the Father's choice to robe his Son in the brokenness of humanity (Phil. 2:7).

It is this lesson that I am learning even as I write this chapter. I bring nothing to the table. I have nothing to offer. I am empty, and it is squarely in that place of destitution that I possess anything for any benefit to anyone. I admit that I know this at least on an intellectual level. It has taken time to transfer that lesson to something as practical as writing this chapter. I suppose I could have learned this lesson at an earlier time. It could have been a sermon I preached or a lesson I taught. It could have been in a board meeting when plans were being made for the future of a local congregation. How did I ever think I had knowledge to offer others who I was convinced were in desperate need of my insight and experience?

I realize now that service without grace is like a Lamborghini without fuel. It may look good, but it is no better than the forgotten clunker in a junkyard. In fact, many may find more satisfaction getting the clunker up and running than sporting the hottest wheels on the road. When I survey the life of Christ, I'm certain that Jesus would have chosen the clunker every time. Maybe that's the point. We may think of ourselves as the

Lamborghini who can bring a lot to the table. Instead, we are more like the clunker that has been relegated to the island of misfit toys.

But Jesus chose the clunkers. He called fishermen with few skillsets. He chose a tax collector with the reputation of a traitor. He recruited the uneducated to counsel the scholars of their day. He sent a woman shamed by marital infidelity to bear his message to Samaria. He sent a delivered, once-demon-possessed man to testify to the work of God in his life. He chose the average (and maybe below average in some ways) to give birth to the most influential world religion to date.

Today we are no different than the first disciples. We have the reputation of the ill-reputed. We may carry the stigma of an ugly divorce. We may live with the story of a failed ministry. We don't know what we don't know. Most of us are just average people living an average life. And yet the word of grace continues through the likes of us.

Example of Grace from an Angel of Mercy

Giving grace away from the depths of our own brokenness can have many looks. But when what we do originates from the influence of grace, it is a beautiful thing to behold. The Apostle Peter described our service as the "multifaceted grace" of God (1 Pet. 4:10 NASB 1995). That could imply a diversity of color, much like a spectrum of colors that provides a subtle beauty from an artist's creation. Just as art is often relegated to the perceived beauty of the beholder, so it is with grace given from a place of complete destitution making the beauty of God's provision a wonder to behold. I witnessed a circumstance that unveiled the unparalleled beauty of grace when one broken person was served by another from her own sense of brokenness. My wife, Jackie, found herself in just such a circumstance.

Jackie lived apart from her mom for almost 30 years until one day her mother, now an elderly woman, called unexpectedly. She announced that she was moving to our area to live by us so we could take care of her. Her decision to move close by greatly impacted Jackie because as a young girl, she was often left to fend for herself. The scars of neglect and abandonment were deeply embedded in her heart. Her mom was a very loving person but lived life pursuing what she enjoyed, often at the expense of her children. By her own admission, she lived apart from God most of her life. So when she moved to our town, she often impersonally referred to God as "the man upstairs."

What we didn't realize at the time was that God was setting up a "but God" moment when my wife and her mom would have the chance to find forgiveness and healing. Jackie's mom was able to see our devotion to God, which often led to spiritual conversations about faith, forgiveness, and healing of her own wounds. They had many conversations that were very difficult and emotionally traumatic. They shed tears. And in the end, before her mom passed away, they found healing and forgiveness that would have otherwise been impossible without God arranging this season of three years to rebuild a damaged and distant relationship.

Caring for her mom at the end of her life rested in Jackie's responsibility. She felt unqualified to do what nurses often do for someone literally on a deathbed. She still harbored the wounds of a relationship that caused deep pain that followed her into this unique time of ministry. Her mom had recently given her life to the Lord, which made a tremendous difference in how they communicated and how her mom viewed her own impending death. Jackie found herself being there for a mom who was often not there for her. And she feared she would not have what it would take to bring comfort and peace to her mom.

A few days before Jackie's mom's death, I visited both of them in her mom's house. She was lying unconscious on the bed while Jackie tended to the details that go along with caring for someone in hospice. As I sat at her mom's kitchen table, I saw something I will never forget. As my wife walked away from the table, there was a sense of peace and the presence of God on her that was as real as any moment in my life. I saw an innocent beauty in my wife in that moment that came from serving in a place of brokenness. She often conveyed how she had nothing to offer, but yet it was in that place of dependence that she found the ability to quietly serve her mom. It was a place where Jackie experienced union and love from God that was selflessly shared with a dear woman on her deathbed.

God didn't choose a pastor or a priest with the experience or knowledge to serve her mom in those closing days. He chose the one person whose wounds should have deemed her incapable of caring. God called the one who carried the offenses like a weight on her shoulders and a smoldering fire in a wounded heart. God chose a broken one to introduce grace to the heart of a wounded woman. He appointed a daughter hurt by neglect to share his grace with the one who did the neglecting. Her mom experienced grace from God, made possible by the grace Jackie gave her as she prepared to meet her God. And it was through the brokenness of my wife that it was possible for the presence of God to give her mom incredible peace up to the very moment when he ushered her home for eternity. What a beautiful moment that was, all made possible because Jackie had nothing to give apart from what Christ had chosen to do for her mom.

My wife felt completely unqualified to be there for a mom who was not there for her. But what if that's the point? What if grace means that God uses us at our worst to bring out the best for someone else?

CHAPTER 5

Myth: If I become a better person, then God will bless me with a better life.

What if grace means ...

Enjoying God is more important than pleasing God.

If your story is like mine, then most likely you live pestered by the stress and anxiety of feeling you've never measured up to God. Unfortunately, anxiety can be the defining emotion of our Christian lives if we have been trapped by performing for God for any length of time. Stress and anxiety deprive us of the peace we seek and make enjoying life with God a far-fetched idea with little relevance. Enjoying God is not a new thought. Scripture assumes that God's people can enjoy him, a life that is possible by living under the influence of grace. Look at these verses to see how they connect our enjoyment of God with grace.

> Rejoice *in the Lord always. I will say it again:*
> *Rejoice!*
>
> —Phil. 4:4

Here is an interesting fact about this verse. The word used for rejoice (Greek: *chairo*) comes from the same Greek word for grace (*charis*), which means enjoyment may just be the ultimate outcome of living under the influence of grace. You will see this trend in the following verses, both from the Old and New Testaments.

> *This is the day that the Lord has made; let us rejoice* [Hebrew: *geel*] *and be glad* [Hebrew: *samach*] *in it.*
>
> —Ps. 118:24

The Hebrew words for rejoice (*samach, geel, ranan*) provide a connection to the Greek word for rejoice (*chairo*), closely linking by association a Hebrew understanding of rejoicing to the influence of grace.

> *Nehemiah said, "Go and enjoy choice food and sweet drinks, and send some to those who have nothing prepared. This day is holy to our LORD. Do not grieve, for the joy of the LORD is your strength.*
>
> —Neh. 8:10

The Hebrew word for joy (*chedvah*) has connections to the Greek's use of the word for rejoice (*chairo*), which, as indicated above, comes from the same word family as the Greek word for grace (*charis*).

*I have told you this so that my joy may be in you and
that your joy may be complete.*

—John 15:11

The Greek word for joy (*chara*) comes from the same
Greek word used in Philippians 4:4 (*chairo*), both words being
connected to grace.

*You make known to me the path of life; you will fill
me with joy in your presence, with eternal pleasures at
your right hand.*

—Ps. 16:11

The Hebrew word for joy (*simchah*) comes from the root
samach from a family of Hebrew words that correspond to the
Greek word for rejoice (*chairo*) and, by association, the Greek
word for grace (*charis*).

I have missed this connection between joy and grace for most
of my Christian life. If enjoyment were a serious consideration
for me at any point in my Christian experience, I am sure I
would have concluded that my lack of enjoyment was due to
my lack of faithfulness. But David reminds us that enjoying the
presence of God comes from God relating to us along our path
of life (Ps. 16:11). Our enjoyment of God has nothing to do
with our faithfulness to him but rather his faithfulness to us. I
don't think enjoying God is what we set out to do, but it does
represent the outcome when we live in peace with God, others,
and ourselves. Those of us with a performance mindset miss out
on enjoying God because we never really experience peace with
God from constantly striving to please him.

The more we consider the connections of God's grace to other aspects of our lives, as the above verses illustrate, the more likely we will enjoy life by finding peace with him and experiencing peace of mind. Isaiah 26:3 (ESV) says, "You keep him in perfect peace whose mind is stayed on you, because he trusts in you." That precious commodity of peace that seems ever so difficult to grasp comes from focusing on God's faithfulness to follow through on every promise he has made.

I believe it is peace—peace with God, peace in our relationships with those around us, peace within ourselves— that represents the deeper motivation for our effort. It is by experiencing peace that we can enjoy God. If peace is the goal we strive for, the performance mindset keeps it out of reach in all aspects of our lives. We don't have peace with God because we can never be sure if our latest efforts rectified our shortcomings. We don't have peace of mind because the memories of past sins and the weight of never knowing if we've done enough to please God result in constant anxiety and stress. And the people around us—our families, friends, churches—will suffer from the emotions caused by that gnawing sense of guilt.

The Sweet Spot for Peace with God, Others, and Ourselves

There is no possible way to enjoy the Christian life without peace. Our enjoyment from knowing him is the ideal life that God has always wanted for us (Ps. 16:11). That enjoyment comes from a state of peace that Scripture describes as rest. The writer of Hebrews describes this rest as a place of peace with God based on his work in us and not our own (Heb. 4:10). I imagine this rest like a deep sigh of relief just before taking a long winter's nap. My eyes close. My heartbeat slows. My body relaxes. The work is done for the moment. My body is tired, but my heart is at peace. It's a perfect combination for a long, restful nap.

That is precisely the idea the writer of Hebrews conveys. The word for rest (Greek: *katapausis*) depicts a cessation of striving. It is rest that is best experienced when it is found in the pleasure of knowing God as the one who did all the work to make peace possible. No longer is there work to be done. We can breathe a deep sigh of relief because Christ did everything that was required by God.

The ideal life God has for each of us is much different than the striving associated with a performance mindset. It is a life that is marked by the perfect work of God in very imperfect people living very imperfect lives. It is a life of peace that cannot be explained away or dismissed by human logic (Phil. 4:6–7). It is a life I call the sweet spot, which I introduced in an earlier chapter. This sweet spot is not dependent on emotions or based on anything we can do or should do. It is not defined by any certain lifestyle or circumstance. This sweet spot is experienced by God's grace and favor influencing all aspects of our lives. Our daily decisions, our relationships, our work, and any other aspect of life are the laboratory for grace to be received and enjoyed. It is where God intended us to live.

It is in the sweet spot of life where the influence of grace has its most lasting effects on how we relate to God and each other. The story of Adam and Eve illustrates what living in that sweet spot is like. At one point in their story after they sinned, we find God walking in the Garden while they hid themselves from his presence. We read that God called out to them, "Where are you?" (Gen. 3:9). This is a significant question because it reveals what their everyday relationship may have been like with each other and God under the influence of his favor.

Before the fall, they enjoyed perfect harmony with God, relating to him as they shared walks and conversations together. They viewed him as relatable and approachable. There is no hint that they related to him as a harsh judge, and the Scriptures doesn't imply that God saw them as subservient to his holiness. There seemed to be a union between them that was indicative of an intimate bond that Adam and Eve were allowed to enjoy, simply because God decided to bless them with that access.

We also know that there was no shame or guilt before the fall (Gen. 2:25). There were no unwanted memories to rehearse. They didn't seem too busy working to keep their access open to God. And God's holiness was the same then as it is today. His law, though not given at the time, still governed human behavior and relationships long before God gave the Ten Commandments to Moses (Gen. 2:3, 7:2–3, 20:3–9, 26:5, Rom. 5:13–14). Shame and guilt were not in God's original plan for humanity, and those emotions were not part of Adam and Eve's experience before they sinned.

The first man and woman seemed to be living in the fullness of everything God had chosen to give them (Gen. 2:7). He gave them purpose in the Garden (Gen. 2:19) and provided a relationship for them that was reminiscent of the harmony and unity reflected in the triune godhead (Gen. 1:26–27, 2:18, Col. 1:19). They lived with the significance of being the instruments by whom all creation lived in harmony with one another (Gen. 2:20).

If mere words could define this sweet spot, then I suggest that Adam and Eve lived with perfect fulfillment, a sense of peace and purpose, meaningful relationships with God and each other, and the significance that they were part of a larger purpose that originated with the plan of God. In essence, they were living under the influence of God's favor and steadfast love in their everyday lives in the Garden.

Does that not sound like what we all strive for? The sweet spot under grace was what God intended for Adam and Eve, and it is what God wants for you and me. We want peace with God in all facets of life. But to find peace, we often strive with God and others from a deep desire to express our love for him through what we do. We strive for peace from anxiety and stress when we fail to meet our own expectations to please God. We seek wholeness when our hearts quake from deep-seated doubts and our minds are distracted by the trouble we constantly try to manage on our own. We long for health and well-being for our marriages, children, and churches as we try to fix our marriages, save our children, and lead our churches. Though all this may be shortsighted, I am convinced that it comes from a heart that desires God and longs for peace of mind.

The Intersection of Grace and Mercy Where We Can Enjoy God

I wonder where all this activity comes from. How can we enjoy peace with God when we struggle every day to find peace in our own hearts? While grace means that nothing else is required from us, we often believe that surely there is something else we need to do to enjoy what God has promised.

Paul suggested that we can possess all God promised us by accessing grace (Rom. 5:2). But that may be easier said than done for those of us with a performance mindset. Our access to grace is much like meeting a stranger at the front door of our home. Where we live represents everything we know. But unknown to us, this unfamiliar person at our door holds in their hand a gift from the Publisher's Clearing House that has the potential to change our lives as we know it. When that person of promise knocks, we can open the door to access the prize they hold in their hand. But if we don't know the person, then we're prone to never open the door to receive the prize.

In like manner, when grace comes knocking (Rev. 3:20), we consider opening ourselves to the possibility of relinquishing control to God. But we hesitate because everything that is familiar to us has been dependent on our own efforts, what we know, and who has earned our trust. But if we open the door, God holds every gift of heaven, ready to freely give them to us without conditions.

In Hebrews 4, the author describes how to open the door to grace by resting in the provision of God when the prevailing need of the moment threatens our grip on faith. "Let us then [in our state of weakness] approach God's throne of grace with confidence, so that we may *receive mercy and find grace* to help us in our time of need" (emphasis added) (Heb. 4:16). This verse continues the writer's point from the earlier text on finding God's rest (Heb. 4:1–11). When we don't have rest, it is essential in this state of weakness that we approach God's throne to receive mercy and find grace. It is not coincidence that the rest we can enjoy in Christ comes through the avenue of grace and mercy. Ceasing our work to please God can only be realized through embracing grace and receiving mercy. It is through God's work of grace and his heart of mercy that our life changes from activity to peace, from stress to rest.

The dual work of grace and mercy to produce the peace we strive for is subtle in Scripture, but it is essential to understand how grace and mercy work together to loosen the grip of the performance mindset. One example of where grace, mercy, and peace are referred to in Scripture is before Jesus was born from the song of Zechariah, John the Baptist's father. His song gives us a snapshot of how grace and mercy work together to bring lasting peace. He wrote, "Because of the *tender mercy* of our God, by which the *rising sun will come to us* from heaven to shine on those living in darkness and in the shadow of death, to guide our feet into the *path of peace*" (emphasis added) (Luke 1:78–79).

Notice the italics I added in these verses. Zechariah describes the mercy of God (Greek: *eleos*) as his deep affection for us that comes from the depths of his being. He then alludes to the grace of God as the "rising sun," a metaphor that depicts the permanence and faithfulness of grace as sure as the sun appears in the east each morning (Ps. 113:3, Mal. 4:2, Titus 2:11, 2 Tim. 1:9–10). Finally, he points to peace as the result of the work of God's grace and mercy shining on us to guide our path of life. John the Baptist's father knew that God's mercy for his people was undeniably connected to the influence of his grace, as sure as the sun rising in the morning and as passionate as God's deep-seated mercy that erupts from the depths of his very being. This undeserving priest gave us insight into the absoluteness of grace and the gut-wrenching compassion of God's mercy to bring the peace we long to experience (Luke 1:76–77).

The significance of peace and mercy as partners with grace also highlights the inseparable role of all three provisions of God. The peace of God (Greek: *eirene*) is closely associated with a state of tranquility as if everything is working in harmony. There is no discord, selfishness, or strife, even at times when life is not perfect. Peace, as described by the word *eirene*, is never dependent on circumstances (Phil. 4:7). When bills are unpaid, peace reminds us of the provision of God. When a diagnosis leads to despair, peace calms the worried heart. When a child goes astray, peace believes they will be found. Peace allows a calmness of mind to believe and trust when circumstances don't warrant.

With the performance mindset, harmony and tranquility are rare because we live as if we have the power to choose God. We are relegated to beg for mercy because of an endless barrage of failed works. Peace on the order of what Adam and Eve first enjoyed is what God originally intended. It is what results from God's original intent, not our own. Because the effects of the fall influence how we feel and what we do, our efforts will never allow us to perceive ourselves from a place of grace. They will never compel us to see God as the merciful God he is. The result of this works mindset will always leave peace just outside our reach. Peace requires grace and mercy working together from the heart of God to produce a life lived in the sweet spot.

Mercy (Greek: *eleos*) explains how God's grace plays out in our lives. To show the relationship between grace and mercy, you might think of grace as God giving us the abundant life we don't deserve and mercy as God withholding the justice we do deserve. We can no more influence God's decision to love us by grace and relate to us by mercy than we can influence the rising of the sun. Mercy makes the favor of God real for us. Because of mercy, grace can never be relegated to mere theology. Grace comes from God's nature. Mercy comes from his heart. Grace is his decision. Mercy is his passion. Grace drives God to us, and mercy keeps God from destroying us. Grace is forgiveness when we deserve punishment. It is protection when we deserve offense. It is provision when we deserve abandonment. It is comfort when we deserve heartache. It is intimacy when we deserve distance. It is encouragement when we deserve discouragement. Grace is heaven when we deserve hell.

Because of grace, God will always choose us, and because of mercy, he will always love, forgive, and pursue us. Because of grace, he will always turn toward us, and because of mercy, he will never turn away. His faithfulness is new every morning when we have been faithless (Lam. 3:23). His compassions never grow faint even though we lack compassion for those around us (Lam. 3:22). His provisions never run dry when the darkest days of life loom over us like a low-hanging cloud. We can forever enjoy the sweet spot of life under the influence of grace, not because we have loved him well enough but because of the mercy he demonstrated when he placed on Christ the punishment we so justly deserve (Isa. 53:4–6, Rom. 3:24–25). The final work of the cross made grace and mercy possible for our peace with God and our access into grace as the beloved and chosen of God (Col. 3:12).

Living Under the Influence of Grace and Mercy

So what does enjoying peace with God look like under the influence of grace and mercy? Let me tell you the end of my grace story, or at least where it is today as of the writing of this book. I am still learning to live under the influence of grace. It is a learning process because I have lived most of life with the opposite mindset—believing that God is a God who is holy above all else, demanding absolute holiness from those who choose to follow him. I empowered my freedom to choose to be faithful or not over God's choice to favor me. I overemphasized my faithfulness to God at the neglect of his faithfulness to provide what I needed to follow him (2 Thess. 3:3).

Learning to live under grace is still a process, and I sometimes slip back into a performance mindset. I am finding that changing my mind from pleasing God to enjoying him has required a lot of changes to my thought patterns and lifestyle. I am learning to be okay with not being okay. I have found that changing how I think about God and myself sometimes takes effort. But while we need to expend effort, the energy we spend is not to please God but to enjoy God.

I continue to remind myself of the notable verses and influential authors of Scripture that point me back to what God is doing in me rather than what I have failed to do for him. I remember how God relates to me from a heart of grace and mercy, and it is in that place where I find peace of mind. When I find that place—the sweet spot—I see myself the way God sees me, and that changes how I relate to everyone around me. I am much more prone to believe now that God chose to love me when I gave him every reason not to choose me. That may sound odd to hear from someone who used to preach, but let me be one of the few to tell you that some of the most broken people in the world are preachers. They have been trained to hide it, and because of practice, they have gotten good at putting on that mask. I too am still God's work in progress.

As I learn to live this ideal life, I am experiencing peace unlike any time in my life. I am fully aware every day that God's work in me is not done, and I believe God will complete that work one day when my Jesus returns to receive me home (Phil. 1:6). Though I continue to struggle at times with pride, performance, and guilt, I am much more aware of when I am tempted to obsess with the next ministry conquest. I rarely consider now what might come next or what's in it for me. I am learning to live fully in the moment, anticipating what God has for me on each given day, whether I consider it a good day or a bad day. For the first time in my life, I am less prone to rehearse my failures. Anger no longer controls my emotions, and shame no longer shapes my self-perception. The absolute certainty of God's grace and mercy is freeing me from the constant obligation to do the right things to please God.

But there was a time when I considered that challenging my mindset about the role of grace was not enough to free me from a performance mindset and bring peace to my life. I have lived most of my life as if I cannot enjoy my Christian life. Because I've lived under the stress and anxiety of performing for God, I never had the energy to just enjoy life. Grace is changing that. I have decided to enjoy my life by doing things that draw my attention to God for no other reason than for the joy of it. I knew if I was going to enjoy God from a place of grace and mercy, I needed to start by being more intentional to do the things God allows me to enjoy.

So I started appreciating the simple pleasures of life—those daddy-daughter dates with a girl I am super proud of, a ballgame with my son, enjoying a song with my stepson, or sitting on a couch watching a late-night movie with my wife. I am learning nature and landscape photography because I suspected I had been missing a lot of what God was doing in the world around me. Much to the chagrin of my children, I also bought an e-bike for—well, you guessed it—just for the fun of it. I now use my e-bike on photography excursions to capture all the moments when God displays his wondrous beauty to me in nature.

All this is teaching me to be aware of what God may be doing in each moment. These weren't quick changes. To take photographs well, for instance, I have to be aware of each moment. I have always been focused on the destination, whether it was a trip we were on or a way to think about life. Now, when my wife and I are traveling, I comment on the scenery around us, provoking her to joke, "Where did my husband go?" My personality for most of my life was more akin to Eeyore than Tigger in the famous *Winnie-the-Pooh* storyline. Though I've never been a let's-stop-and-smell-the-roses kind of person, I notice now that I laugh more. With things I once took for granted, I pause now to consider the grace that God may be giving me in the mundaneness of the moment. I can honestly say that grace is leading to all these changes.

You may also pick up some practices to lean into grace, and you may stop others. You may find that you need to lean into reading Scripture or exploring prayer as a more notable practice in your life. Because of my background, I was comfortable exploring grace as I navigated Scripture and read books, considering grace in prayer and conversations. I loosened up on practices like prayer and Scripture reading by changing their purpose rather than the practices themselves. I began to rethink why I read Scripture. I have always tried to prioritize listening to God's voice when I read Scripture, but I usually defaulted to a sense of obligation that motivated my reading. The influence of grace has made listening to God's voice through reading Scripture a much more natural byproduct of a grace-based relationship with him.

Like me, you may think differently over time. You may do different things. Sure, some things may change, some subtle and some not so subtle such as picking up photography or buying an e-bike. Those changes may sound unimportant, but for me, they aren't. They represent a reorganization of my life to enjoy the abundant life God has promised us in Christ. However God leads you to adjust your life to grace, just know that the adjustments you make do not make God love you more or less. God chose to relate to you with favor and lovingkindness long before you ever chose to relate to him. The adjustments we make put us under the influence of his grace and nothing more.

I am certainly not a finished product. I have a long way to go. I still tend toward performance. I am still very cognizant of when I fail spiritually. Even with a changed purpose, I catch myself more often than I'd like to admit reading Scripture as a to-do list to please God. But in that struggle, I have found peace. Even in the struggle, I am learning to consider this: What if grace means that enjoying God is more important than pleasing him?

FINAL THOUGHTS

How do we become influenced by grace? We explore grace. We stop looking to ourselves as the fix or the failure. Like the centurion, we hunt down grace. Like the blind man when abandoned to the side of the road, we listen for the voice of grace. We cry out to grace. We stop pursuing performance to please God. Instead, we pursue grace to enjoy God. We read every word that grace speaks. We write down every thought that leads us to the cool waters of grace. We find our refreshment with grace. We get up close and personal with grace. We come clean with grace. We seek harmony because of grace. We listen for grace in every conversation. We enjoy peace in every smiling face. We pause to notice grace in the small details of life. We embrace mercy when we fall under the trap of temptation. We cling to every verse of Scripture that points us to grace.

Every part of our life, every ambition that drives our misguided passions, every thought that rules our misplaced desires, every speck of shame that reminds us of our failed past, every hint of guilt that weighs us down today, and every regret that clouds our hope for tomorrow fall at the feet of the One who is our grace—Jesus Christ!

Here are a few resources to help you live in this sweet spot where you can find peace, where you can enjoy your life with God every day under the influence of grace. These resources are based on the assumption that the more you interact with every great book and timeless Scripture that points you to grace, the more influential grace will become in your life. I hope you have enjoyed this book, but I also hope you enjoy pursuing grace with the books I've listed below. Happy reading!

- *Praying Grace: 55 Meditations and Declarations on the Finished Work of Christ*, by David Holland
- *The Freedom of Self-Forgetfulness: The Path to True Christian Joy*, by Timothy Keller
- *The Cure: What If God Isn't Who You Think He Is and Neither Are You*, by John Lynch, Bruce McNicol, and Bill Thrall
- *All Is Grace: A Ragamuffin Memoir*, by Brennan Manning
- *The Furious Longing of God*, by Brennan Manning
- *The Ragamuffin Gospel: Good News for the Bedraggled, Beat-Up, and Burnt Out*, by Brennan Manning
- *The Relentless Tenderness of Jesus*, by Brennan Manning
- *Gentle and Lowly: The Heart of Christ for Sinners and Sufferers*, by Dane Ortland
- *The Good and Beautiful God: Falling in Love with the God Jesus Knows*, by James Bryan Smith

As great as all these books have been to bring me under the influence of grace, there is nothing that can compare to the difference that Scripture has made in my life. There are numerous verses you can read and think about that will make a difference in your life for the sake of grace. I have listed only a few that represent the starting point for putting this book together. Think deeply through each verse by considering what God may be showing you about grace. If something strikes you that you don't want to forget, write it down in a journal or notebook. May the words of grace penetrate your heart as you learn from God at his feet (Matt. 11:28–30).

> *Come to me, all you who are weary and burdened, and I will give you rest. Take my yoke upon you and learn from me, for I am gentle and humble in heart, and you will find rest for your souls. For my yoke is easy and my burden is light.*
>
> —Matt. 11:28–30

> *For sin shall no longer be your master, because you are not under the law, but under grace.*
>
> —Rom. 6:14

> *Therefore, my dear friends, as you have always obeyed— not only in my presence, but now much more in my absence—continue to work out your salvation with fear and trembling, for it is God who works in you to will and to act in order to fulfill his good purpose.*
>
> —Phil. 2:12–13

> *So too, at the present time there is a remnant chosen by grace. And if by grace, then it cannot be based on works; if it were, grace would no longer be grace.*
>
> —Rom. 11:5–6

He has saved us and called us to a holy life—not because of anything we have done but because of his own purpose and grace. This grace was given us in Christ Jesus before the beginning of time.

—2 Tim. 1:9

You did not choose me, but I chose you and appointed you so that you might go and bear fruit—fruit that will last—and so that whatever you ask in my name the Father will give you.

—John 15:16

Jesus called them together and said, "You know that the rulers of the Gentiles lord it over them, and their high officials exercise authority over them. Not so with you. Instead, whoever wants to become great among you must be your servant, and whoever wants to be first must be your slave—just as the Son of Man did not come to be served, but to serve, and to give his life as a ransom for many."

—Matt. 20:25–28

Yet to all who did receive him, to those who believed in his name, he gave the right to become children of God—children born not of natural descent, nor of human decision or a husband's will, but born of God.

—John 1:12–13

Therefore, there is now no condemnation for those who are in Christ Jesus.

—Rom. 8:1

But God demonstrates his own love for us in this: While we were still sinners, Christ died for us.

—Rom. 5:8

For just as through the disobedience of the one man the many were made sinners, so also through the obedience of the one man the many will be made righteous.

—Rom. 5:19

God made him who had no sin to be sin for us, so that in him we might become the righteousness of God. As God's co-workers we urge you not to receive God's grace in vain. For he says, "In the time of my favor I heard you, and in the day of salvation I helped you." I tell you, now is the time of God's favor, now is the day of salvation.

—2 Cor. 5:21–6:2

May the grace of the Lord Jesus Christ, and the love of God, and the fellowship of the Holy Spirit be with you all.

—2 Cor. 13:14

www.ingramcontent.com/pod-product-compliance
Lightning Source LLC
LaVergne TN
LVHW051424080426
835508LV00022B/3236